Baby Shower

Welcome Baby Girl

Adorable Baby Picture

Baby Shower Guest Book

Name		Date of Birth	
Day		Time		Weight	

Relationships to Parents	Advice for Parents

Wishes

Resemblance — Mom! — Dad!

Baby Shower Guest Book

Name		Date of Birth	
Day		Time	Weight	

Relationships to Parents

Advice for Parents

Wishes

Resemblance   Mom!   Dad!

Baby Shower Guest Book

Name		Date of Birth	
Day		Time	Weight

Relationships to Parents	Advice for Parents

Wishes

Resemblance   Mom!   Dad!

Baby Shower Guest Book

Name		Date of Birth	
Day		Time		Weight	

Relationships to Parents

Advice for Parents

Wishes

Resemblance   Mom!   Dad!

Baby Shower Guest Book

Name		Date of Birth	

Day		Time		Weight	

Relationships to Parents	Advice for Parents

Wishes

Resemblance   Mom!   Dad!

Baby Shower Guest Book

Name			Date of Birth	
Day		Time		Weight

Relationships to Parents	Advice for Parents

Wishes

Resemblance	Mom!	Dad!

Baby Shower Guest Book

Name		Date of Birth	
Day		Time	Weight	

Relationships to Parents	Advice for Parents

Wishes

Resemblance   Mom!   Dad!

Baby Shower Guest Book

Name		Date of Birth	
Day		Time	Weight

Relationships to Parents	Advice for Parents

Wishes	

Resemblance   Mom!   Dad!

Baby Shower Guest Book

Name		Date of Birth	

Day		Time		Weight	

Relationships to Parents	Advice for Parents

Wishes

Resemblance   Mom!   Dad!

Baby Shower Guest Book

Name		Date of Birth	
Day		Time	Weight

Relationships to Parents

Advice for Parents

Wishes

Resemblance   Mom!   Dad!

Baby Shower Guest Book

| Name | | Date of Birth | |
| Day | | Time | | Weight | |

Relationships to Parents	Advice for Parents

Wishes

Resemblance   Mom!   Dad!

Baby Shower Guest Book

Name		Date of Birth	
Day		Time	Weight

Relationships to Parents

Advice for Parents

Wishes

Resemblance   Mom!   Dad!

Baby Shower Guest Book

Name			Date of Birth	
Day		Time		Weight

Relationships to Parents	Advice for Parents

Wishes	

Resemblance   Mom!   Dad!

Baby Shower Guest Book

Name		Date of Birth	
Day		Time	Weight

Relationships to Parents	Advice for Parents

Wishes

Resemblance   Mom!   Dad!

Baby Shower Guest Book

Name		Date of Birth	
Day		Time	Weight

Relationships to Parents	Advice for Parents

Wishes

Resemblance   Mom!   Dad!

Baby Shower Guest Book

Name		Date of Birth	
Day		Time	Weight

Relationships to Parents

Advice for Parents

Wishes

Resemblance   Mom!   Dad!

Baby Shower Guest Book

Name		Date of Birth	
Day		Time	Weight

Relationships to Parents

Advice for Parents

Wishes	

Resemblance	Mom!	Dad!

Baby Shower Guest Book

Name		Date of Birth	
Day		Time	Weight

Relationships to Parents

Advice for Parents

Wishes

Resemblance   Mom!   Dad!

Baby Shower Guest Book

Name		Date of Birth	
Day		Time	Weight

Relationships to Parents

Advice for Parents

Wishes

Resemblance   Mom!   Dad!

Baby Shower Guest Book

Name		Date of Birth	
Day		Time	Weight

Relationships to Parents	Advice for Parents

Wishes

Resemblance   Mom!   Dad!

Baby Shower Guest Book

Name		Date of Birth	
Day		Time	Weight

Relationships to Parents	Advice for Parents

Wishes

Resemblance   Mom!   Dad!

Baby Shower Guest Book

Name		Date of Birth	
Day		Time		Weight	

Relationships to Parents	Advice for Parents

Wishes	

Resemblance	Mom!	Dad!

Baby Shower Guest Book

Name		Date of Birth	
Day		Time	Weight

Relationships to Parents

Advice for Parents

Wishes

Resemblance   ◯ Mom!   ◯ Dad!

Baby Shower Guest Book

| Name | | Date of Birth | |
| Day | | Time | Weight | |

Relationships to Parents

Advice for Parents

Wishes

Resemblance ◯ Mom! ◯ Dad!

Baby Shower Guest Book

Name		Date of Birth	
Day		Time	Weight

Relationships to Parents	Advice for Parents

Wishes	

Resemblance   Mom!   Dad!

Baby Shower Guest Book

Name		Date of Birth	
Day		Time	Weight

Relationships to Parents	Advice for Parents

Wishes

Resemblance   Mom!   Dad!

Baby Shower Guest Book

Name		Date of Birth	
Day		Time	Weight	

Relationships to Parents	Advice for Parents

Wishes	

Resemblance	Mom!	Dad!

Baby Shower Guest Book

| Name | | Date of Birth | |
| Day | | Time | | Weight | |

| Relationships to Parents | Advice for Parents |

Wishes

Resemblance   Mom!   Dad!

Baby Shower Guest Book

Name		Date of Birth	
Day		Time		Weight	

Relationships to Parents	Advice for Parents

Wishes	

Resemblance	Mom!	Dad!

Baby Shower Guest Book

Name		Date of Birth	
Day		Time	Weight

Relationships to Parents	Advice for Parents

Wishes

Resemblance   Mom!   Dad!

Baby Shower Guest Book

Name		Date of Birth	
Day		Time		Weight	

Relationships to Parents	Advice for Parents

Wishes	

Resemblance	Mom!	Dad!

Baby Shower Guest Book

Name		Date of Birth	
Day		Time	Weight

Relationships to Parents

Advice for Parents

Wishes

Resemblance   Mom!   Dad!

Baby Shower Guest Book

Name		Date of Birth	
Day		Time		Weight	

Relationships to Parents	Advice for Parents

Wishes

Resemblance Mom! Dad!

Baby Shower Guest Book

Name		Date of Birth	
Day		Time	Weight

Relationships to Parents

Advice for Parents

Wishes

Resemblance   ○ Mom!   ○ Dad!

Baby Shower Guest Book

Name		Date of Birth	
Day		Time		Weight	

Relationships to Parents	Advice for Parents

Wishes	

Resemblance   Mom!   Dad!

Baby Shower Guest Book

Name		Date of Birth	
Day		Time	Weight

Relationships to Parents	Advice for Parents

Wishes

Resemblance   Mom!   Dad!

Baby Shower Guest Book

Name			Date of Birth	
Day		Time	Weight	

Relationships to Parents	Advice for Parents

Wishes

Resemblance · Mom! · Dad!

Baby Shower Guest Book

Name		Date of Birth	
Day		Time	Weight	

Relationships to Parents

Advice for Parents

Wishes

Resemblance   Mom!   Dad!

Baby Shower Guest Book

Name		Date of Birth	

Day		Time		Weight	

Relationships to Parents	Advice for Parents

Wishes

Resemblance ◯ Mom! ◯ Dad!

Baby Shower Guest Book

Name		Date of Birth	
Day		Time	Weight

Relationships to Parents	Advice for Parents

Wishes

Resemblance   Mom!   Dad!

Baby Shower Guest Book

Name		Date of Birth	
Day		Time	Weight

Relationships to Parents

Advice for Parents

Wishes

Resemblance   Mom!   Dad!

Baby Shower Guest Book

Name		Date of Birth	
Day		Time	Weight

Relationships to Parents	Advice for Parents

Wishes

Resemblance   ◯ Mom!   ◯ Dad!

Baby Shower Guest Book

Name		Date of Birth	
Day		Time	Weight

Relationships to Parents	Advice for Parents

Wishes	

Resemblance   Mom!   Dad!

Baby Shower Guest Book

Name		Date of Birth	
Day		Time	Weight

Relationships to Parents

Advice for Parents

Wishes

Resemblance   Mom!   Dad!

Baby Shower Guest Book

Name		Date of Birth	

Day		Time		Weight	

Relationships to Parents	Advice for Parents

Wishes	

Resemblance	Mom!	Dad!

Baby Shower Guest Book

Name		Date of Birth	
Day		Time	Weight	

Relationships to Parents

Advice for Parents

Wishes

Resemblance — Mom! — Dad!

Baby Shower Guest Book

| Name | | Date of Birth | |
| Day | | Time | | Weight | |

Relationships to Parents	Advice for Parents

| Wishes | |

| Resemblance | Mom! | Dad! |

Baby Shower Guest Book

Name		Date of Birth	
Day		Time	Weight

Relationships to Parents

Advice for Parents

Wishes

Resemblance   Mom!   Dad!

Baby Shower Guest Book

Name		Date of Birth	

Day		Time		Weight	

Relationships to Parents	Advice for Parents

Wishes	

Resemblance	Mom!	Dad!

Baby Shower Guest Book

Name		Date of Birth	
Day		Time	Weight

Relationships to Parents

Advice for Parents

Wishes

Resemblance	Mom!	Dad!

Baby Shower Guest Book

| Name | | Date of Birth | |
| Day | | Time | Weight |

Relationships to Parents	Advice for Parents

Wishes

| Resemblance | ◯ Mom! | ◯ Dad! |

Baby Shower Guest Book

| Name | | Date of Birth | |
| Day | | Time | Weight |

| Relationships to Parents | Advice for Parents |

Wishes

Resemblance   Mom!   Dad!

Baby Shower Guest Book

| Name | | Date of Birth | |
| Day | | Time | Weight |

Relationships to Parents

Advice for Parents

Wishes

Resemblance — Mom! — Dad!

Baby Shower Guest Book

Name		Date of Birth	
Day		Time	Weight

Relationships to Parents	Advice for Parents

Wishes

Resemblance	Mom!	Dad!

Baby Shower Guest Book

Name		Date of Birth	
Day		Time	Weight

Relationships to Parents

Advice for Parents

Wishes

Resemblance   Mom!   Dad!

Baby Shower Guest Book

Name		Date of Birth	
Day	Time	Weight	

Relationships to Parents	Advice for Parents

Wishes

Resemblance   ◯ **Mom!**   ◯ **Dad!**

Baby Shower Guest Book

Name		Date of Birth	
Day		Time	Weight

Relationships to Parents	Advice for Parents

Wishes

Resemblance   Mom!   Dad!

Baby Shower Guest Book

Name			Date of Birth	
Day		Time	Weight	

Relationships to Parents	Advice for Parents

Wishes

Resemblance	◯ Mom!	◯ Dad!

Baby Shower Guest Book

Name		Date of Birth	
Day		Time		Weight	

Relationships to Parents	Advice for Parents

Wishes

Resemblance   Mom!   Dad!

Baby Shower Guest Book

Name		Date of Birth	
Day		Time	Weight

Relationships to Parents

Advice for Parents

Wishes

Resemblance | Mom! | Dad!

Baby Shower Guest Book

| Name | | Date of Birth | |
| Day | | Time | Weight | |

Relationships to Parents	Advice for Parents

Wishes

Resemblance   Mom!   Dad!

Baby Shower Guest Book

Name		Date of Birth	
Day		Time	Weight	

Relationships to Parents	Advice for Parents

Wishes

Resemblance	◯ Mom!	◯ Dad!

Baby Shower Guest Book

Name		Date of Birth	
Day		Time	Weight

Relationships to Parents

Advice for Parents

Wishes

Resemblance Mom! Dad!

Baby Shower Guest Book

Name		Date of Birth	
Day		Time	Weight

Relationships to Parents

Advice for Parents

Wishes	

Resemblance	Mom!	Dad!

Baby Shower Guest Book

Name		Date of Birth	
Day		Time		Weight	

Relationships to Parents	Advice for Parents

Wishes

Resemblance Mom! Dad!

Baby Shower Guest Book

Name		Date of Birth	

Day		Time		Weight	

Relationships to Parents	Advice for Parents

Wishes	

Resemblance	Mom!	Dad!

Baby Shower Guest Book

Name		Date of Birth	
Day	Time	Weight	

Relationships to Parents	Advice for Parents

Wishes

Resemblance	Mom!	Dad!

Baby Shower Guest Book

Name		Date of Birth	

Day		Time		Weight	

Relationships to Parents	Advice for Parents

Wishes

Resemblance   Mom!   Dad!

Baby Shower Guest Book

Name		Date of Birth	
Day		Time	Weight

Relationships to Parents	Advice for Parents

Wishes

Resemblance   Mom!   Dad!

Baby Shower Guest Book

Name		Date of Birth	
Day		Time	Weight

Relationships to Parents	Advice for Parents

Wishes

Resemblance	Mom!	Dad!

Baby Shower Guest Book

| Name | | Date of Birth | |
| Day | | Time | Weight |

Relationships to Parents

Advice for Parents

Wishes

Resemblance — Mom! — Dad!

Baby Shower Guest Book

| Name | | Date of Birth | |
| Day | | Time | Weight | |

Relationships to Parents

Advice for Parents

Wishes

Resemblance   Mom!   Dad!

Baby Shower Guest Book

Name		Date of Birth	
Day		Time		Weight	

Relationships to Parents	Advice for Parents

Wishes

Resemblance   Mom!   Dad!

Baby Shower Guest Book

| Name | | Date of Birth | |
| Day | | Time | | Weight | |

Relationships to Parents	Advice for Parents

Wishes

Resemblance   Mom!   Dad!

Baby Shower Guest Book

| Name | | Date of Birth | |
| Day | | Time | | Weight | |

Relationships to Parents	Advice for Parents

Wishes

Resemblance   Mom!   Dad!

Baby Shower Guest Book

Name		Date of Birth	
Day		Time		Weight	

Relationships to Parents	Advice for Parents

Wishes	

Resemblance   Mom!   Dad!

Baby Shower Guest Book

Name		Date of Birth	
Day		Time	Weight

Relationships to Parents	Advice for Parents

Wishes

Resemblance   Mom!   Dad!

Baby Shower Guest Book

| Name | | | Date of Birth | |
| Day | | Time | Weight | |

Relationships to Parents	Advice for Parents

| Wishes | |

| Resemblance | Mom! | Dad! |

Baby Shower Guest Book

Name		Date of Birth	
Day	Time	Weight	

Relationships to Parents	Advice for Parents

Wishes

Resemblance ⚪ **Mom!** ⚪ **Dad!**

Baby Shower Guest Book

Name		Date of Birth	
Day		Time	Weight

Relationships to Parents

Advice for Parents

Wishes

Resemblance   ◯ Mom!   ◯ Dad!

Baby Shower Guest Book

| Name | | Date of Birth | |
| Day | | Time | Weight |

Relationships to Parents	Advice for Parents

Wishes

Resemblance   Mom!   Dad!

Baby Shower Guest Book

Name		Date of Birth	
Day		Time	Weight

Relationships to Parents	Advice for Parents

Wishes

Resemblance   Mom!   Dad!

Baby Shower Guest Book

Name		Date of Birth	
Day		Time	Weight

Relationships to Parents	Advice for Parents

Wishes	

Resemblance	Mom!	Dad!

Baby Shower Guest Book

Name		Date of Birth	
Day		Time	Weight

Relationships to Parents	Advice for Parents

Wishes

Resemblance	Mom!	Dad!

Baby Shower Guest Book

Name		Date of Birth	

Day		Time		Weight	

Relationships to Parents	Advice for Parents

Wishes

Resemblance	Mom!	Dad!

Baby Shower Guest Book

Name		Date of Birth	
Day		Time	Weight

Relationships to Parents	Advice for Parents

Wishes

Resemblance   Mom!   Dad!

Baby Shower Guest Book

| Name | | Date of Birth | |
| Day | | Time | Weight | |

Relationships to Parents

Advice for Parents

Wishes

Resemblance Mom! Dad!

Baby Shower Guest Book

Name		Date of Birth	

Day		Time		Weight	

Relationships to Parents	Advice for Parents

Wishes

Resemblance — **Mom!**   **Dad!**

Baby Shower Guest Book

Name		Date of Birth	
Day		Time		Weight	

Relationships to Parents	Advice for Parents

Wishes

Resemblance   Mom!   Dad!

Funny Photos

Funny Photos

Funny Photos

Funny Photos

Funny Photos

Funny Photos

Thank you !

We would really appreciate your feedback, please send us a email to:

ritirra@gmail.com